YOUR DOCTOR
MY DOCTOR

YOUR DOCTOR

MY DOCTOR

Written and illustrated by
JOAN DRESCHER

WALKER AND COMPANY ✸ New York

DEDICATION

For
the special women of visions,
the many health professionals, and the doctors
who gave freely of their time.
To
Ken, my husband, and Jeanne, my editor:
all healers, helpers, and friends.

First published in the United States of America in 1987 by the Walker Publishing Company, Inc.

Published simultaneously in Canada by John Wiley & Sons Canada, Limited, Rexdale, Ontario

Library of Congress Cataloging-in-Publication Data

Drescher, Joan E.
  Your doctor, my doctor.

  1. Physicians—Juvenile literature.   I. Title.
R707.D74   1987   610.69'52   86-22449
ISBN 0-8027-6668-4
ISBN 0-8027-6669-2 (lib. bdg.)

Printed in the United States of America

10   9   8   7   6   5   4   3   2   1

Doctors are real people, just like you and me.

They have families and pets. They ride bikes and have picnics.

Doctors who learn in hospitals are called interns and residents. Medical students go to school in the hospital. They have to do homework and pass tests.

Sometimes doctors get sick, just like you do. What do you think they do?

They call a doctor.

Doctors can be women or men. They can be old or young, and they all have names, just like you and me. Their job is to help you get well and stay well.

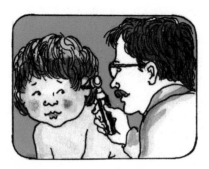

An ear, nose, and throat doctor can help your earache.

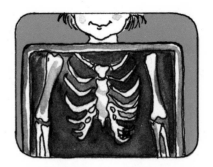

A radiologist studies X-rays to find out what you're like on the inside.

A hematologist studies your blood.

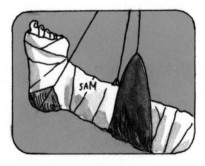

An orthopedist repairs your broken bones.

A surgeon performs operations.

Some doctors are specialists. Here are just a few.

When you were born, an obstetrician or midwife probably helped with your birth.

And as you grew, a pediatrician (a doctor who only treats children) looked after you.

Kim was afraid to visit the doctor. She was sure he would hurt her, so she hid under the desk in the waiting room.

The doctor told Kim that it was all right to feel frightened. Then he showed her his stethoscope; he let her listen to her own heartbeat with it. She tried it out on Sam. When the doctor gave Kim a booster shot, she winced, but she decided it wasn't so bad after all.

Billy broke his leg playing hockey. At the hospital an X-ray technician took a picture of Billy's leg, and a radiologist read his X-ray.

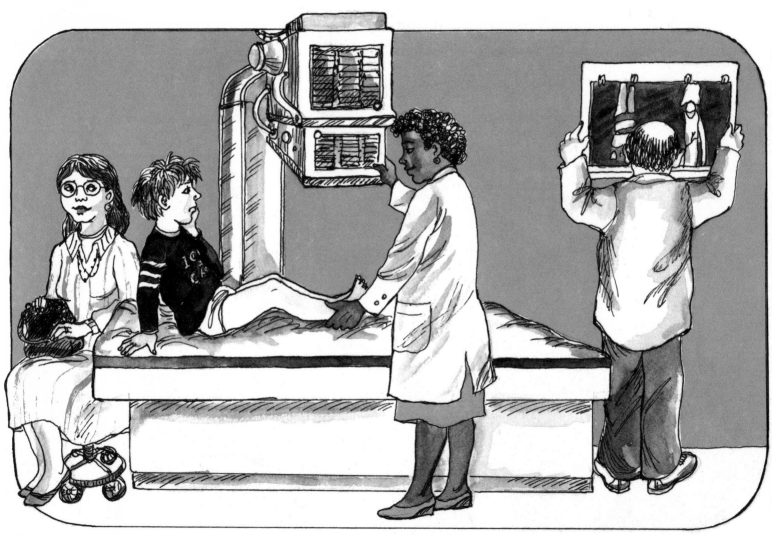

A doctor called an orthopedic surgeon set the bone and put a cast on Billy's leg to protect it while the bone healed. All the kids in Billy's class wrote their names on his cast.

Sam was riding on Mark's handlebars when they skidded and fell. Sam's leg was bleeding badly, so Mark ran to a neighbor's house and called an ambulance. Then he called Sam's mother.

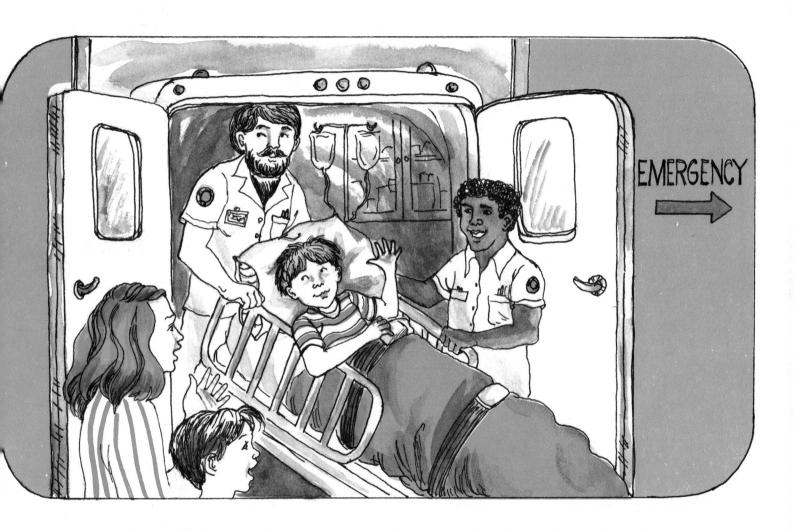

When the ambulance arrived, a paramedic knew exactly what to do until they got to the hospital. Sam's mother got there almost as fast as they did. Sam got sixteen stitches.

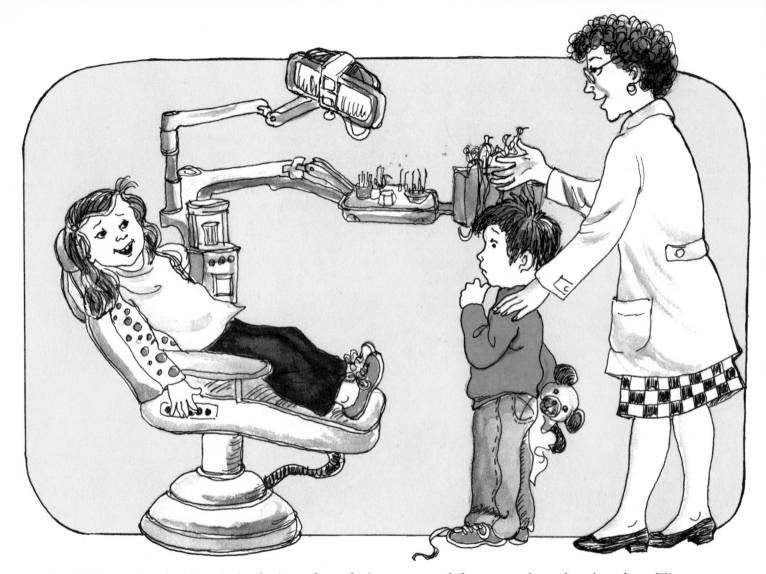

Sally sat in the dentist's chair and made it go up and down to show her brother, Tim. She wasn't always so brave, but she learned to trust Dr. Lisa, and now she doesn't mind having her teeth filled.

Doctors who help us when we have trouble with our eyes are called ophthalmologists and optometrists. Ben could not read the blackboard. The eye doctor tested Ben's eyes and decided that he needed glasses. Ben did not like the idea, but he liked finding frames that looked like his favorite rock star's. Now everything looks clearer, especially the blackboard.

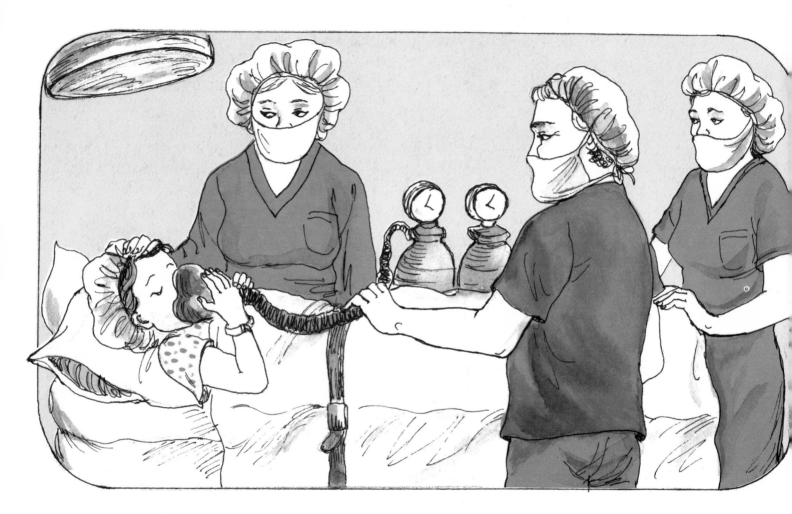

Liz had to have her tonsils removed. At the hospital, a doctor called an anesthesiologist put a mask over her nose and mouth and told her to count to ten. Before Liz got to ten, she fell asleep. When she woke up, she was surprised that it was all over and that her tonsils were out. She had counted only to seven.

Amy and Doctor Ted are old friends. She has been coming to this hospital for surgery ever since she was small, and he has always taken care of her. Dr. Ted and the hospital staff had a surprise birthday party for Amy. She would like to be a surgeon when she grows up.

Judy's father lost his job, and he and Judy's mother were always fighting. Judy felt sad and angry, but she could not cry like the baby or scream like the older kids. She was so frightened she could not even talk about how she felt.

Doctors can help us when our bodies get sick, but there are also doctors who help us when we feel sad, angry, upset, or helpless. These doctors are called psychiatrists and therapists.

Judy's family finally met with a psychiatrist. At first Judy wondered if she would get a shot or if Dr. Brown would hurt her. Instead, her family learned to talk about the things that were really bothering them. With Dr. Brown's help, they learned not only to listen to one another, but to care about each other's feelings. Things are much better for Judy and her family now.

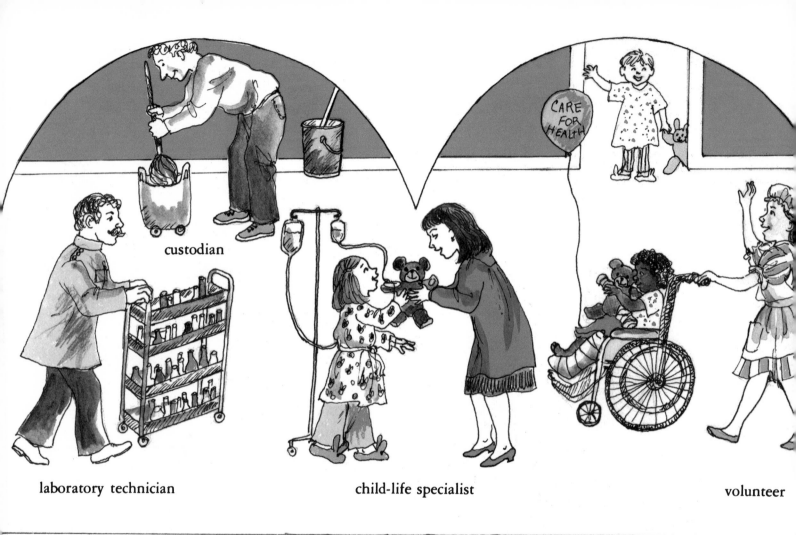

custodian

laboratory technician

child-life specialist

volunteer

Caring is important to your health. There are many people who care for you along with doctors in the hospital. Here are just a few.

Nurses are always there, caring for you night and day when you are in the hospital.
Your Mom and Dad may be able to stay overnight to help care for you, too.

We all know that staying healthy means eating the right foods and getting enough sleep and exercise.

But did you know that worrying a lot and feeling tense and angry can make us sick?

Our bodies work much better when we are happy, relaxed, and loving.

Listen to your body. It can tell you a lot. And remember to tell your doctor what's bothering you. Doctors need your help in keeping you healthy and happy.

SELF-PRONOUNCING INDEX

p-18,19	ambulance	<u>am</u> bew lans
p-22	anesthesiologist	an es thee zi <u>ahl</u> o gist
p-15	booster	<u>boos</u> ter
p-26	child-life specialist	child life <u>spesh</u> al ist
p-26	custodian	cus <u>toe</u> di an
p-20	dentist	<u>den</u> tist
p-11	hematologist	hee mah <u>tahl</u> o gist
p-7	intern	<u>inn</u> tern
p-26	laboratory technician	<u>lab</u> ra toree teck <u>nish</u> un
p-12	midwife	<u>mid</u> wife
p-12	obstetrician	ob sta <u>trish</u> en
p-21	ophthalmologist	opp tha <u>mol</u> o gist
p-21	optometrist	opp <u>tom</u> o trist
p-17	orthopedic surgeon	or tho <u>peed</u> ic <u>sir</u> jen
p-11	orthopedist	or tho <u>peed</u> ist
p-13	paramedic	par a <u>med</u> ik
p-13	pediatrician	peed ee a <u>trish</u> en
p-24	psychiatrist	sy <u>ki</u> a trist
p-11,16	radiologist	ray dee <u>ol</u> o gist
p-7,19	resident doctor	<u>res</u> i dent <u>dok</u> tur
p-16	stethoscope	<u>steth</u> o scope
p-11,23	surgeon	<u>sir</u> jen
p-24	therapist	<u>ther</u> a pist
p-26	volunteer	vol un <u>teer</u>
p-16	X-ray technician	X-ray teck <u>nish</u> en